# THE WINNING CV
## AN ESSENTIAL GUIDE TO DEVELOPING A PROFESSIONAL CV

Unlock Your Potential
Brand Yourself To Win

Sharon Khosa

EARN COMPETITIVE ADVANTAGE & LAND AN INTERVIEW!

ISBN: 978-0-620-88096-1
eBook: 978-1-77605-674-3

Editor: Khotso Pekane
vowpekane@gmail.com

Typesetting by Janet Von Kleist
jvonkleist@yahoo.com

Published by Kwarts Publishers
www.kwartspublishers.co.za

Contact the Author:
sharon@elitesuccess.co.za

# *Acknowledgements*

The quality of one's life is determined by the quality of relationships that one builds, and the people that are part of those life moments. Life would really be insignificant and have no true meaning if it was to be lived alone. I am who I am today because there are people in my life that help me to build, to enjoy and experience life the way I do and to live a truly meaningful life. Without the support of all these people, my life would truly not be what it is and I doubt that I would wake up every morning with an intention to do, to be and to become a better version of myself.

My kids, Nyiko, Blessed, Vunene and Lulama. You all give me a reason to wake up every morning and do my best. I hope that this book will be worth reading to you and the generations that will follow. Special thanks to my first born, Nyiko, for the little push and re-assurance that this information was indeed worth sharing.

To my mother, Nkhensane Khosa, for always believing in my dreams no matter how crazy they seem, for always supporting me to the best of your ability, Nakhensa Mhani. To my editors, you are the best! I truly value your support and thank you for challenging me to give this book my utmost best. And finally, to everyone reading this book: I believe you will find the value that you deserve and most importantly, the help that you require in landing that much needed interview and ultimately your dream Job. I believe in you, I believe in your dreams, I believe you will get the Job of your dreams and most importantly live a purpose driven life. **I wish you all of the best in your journey of success!**

# CONTENTS

# PREFACE

There are two types of job seekers: Those who land an interview but never make it past the interview stage and also those who never land the interview at all. We are expected to know the how's and what's of a CV as well as our potential employers' expectations, yet we do not get enough academic exposure in this aspect. A CV is that one component that determines your fate in the job market. Unfortunately, most CV's never make it to the short-listing tables and this is generally because they are either not professional enough or they don't represent us well enough.

A Curriculum Vitae is the most important tool in the life of a professional. A CV on its own can determine how far you will go in meeting your professional aspirations and how much of your potential you fulfil. Yet, this very pertinent aspect of our lives is not being given the attention it so desperately deserves in our academic institutions, leaving us to fill in the gaps left by what is most often twelve years of schooling. This tool holds the power to influence how your potential employers view you. Not only that, but it is very often the determining factor in whether you land that interview or not.

The secret formula to winning in the job market and landing the job of your dreams is determined by two important factors: The first is how well structured and developed your CV is and the second is how well you do during your interview. This book is meant to assist you in landing that much needed interview. My follow up book **Job Interview Success Secrets** will help you navigate through the interview with ease. Used together, these two books can significantly increase your chances of landing the job of your dreams.

So, whether you are just starting out or transitioning into a new field, your CV will determine how far you go in meeting your dreams and aspirations. This book is for everyone who wants to improve their CV writing skills in such a way that will cause them to stand out. It seeks to assist individuals who are looking to get more out of their professional lives, get noticed by potential employers or even to get that much wanted promotion. Whether you are a novice professional, a growing professional, a new graduate, a matriculant or even a primary level scholar: this guide is essential for you.

It is greatly important that children learn how to represent themselves from a very young age. I highly recommend that individuals begin to learn how to develop a CV that best represents them from their primary level of schooling. This will prepare them for the job market and open plenty doors of opportunities by the time they obtain a skill or a qualification. Remember, personal presentation is never taught as part of any subject in school in an effort to maximise chances of employment and business opportunities. I encourage school leaving pupils to know how to develop a professional CV but even better, learn how to present themselves in a profitable manner in order to get them ready to enter the job market or to go into business. Every one of us needs a CV that can represent us effectively and I believe that this tool will help you get just that.

**I hope that this book can lead you to success in landing that interview, get you into your dream job, and most importantly help you to discover your life's purpose.**

# INTRODUCTION

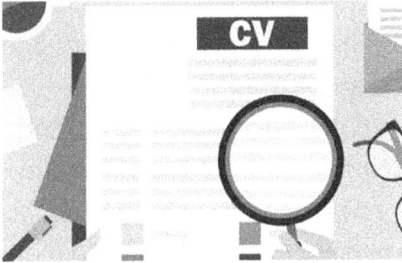

It was just few months before I started with my final year examinations at the University of Limpopo. "This is it, I am going to write my final examination and soon after this I will be out there looking for employment opportunities." This is what I thought and I was asking myself if I was ready for the unknown journey ahead. The reality was that I was not completely ready. Every time I cast my eyes into the future and imagined my pending employment, I became anxious. All I knew was that at the end of that year I would have a qualification, and nothing more. I was oblivious as to what skills were required for the job I was going to get into or even what skills I had.

The reality was that if I were to go into the job market I would need a CV. Then, like a sudden rain drop under a clear blue sky, it hit me: "How do I even begin developing one?" What followed this realization was a journey of learning how to develop my own CV. I needed to go beyond just writing a CV; I had to go through a personal assessment journey in order to assess my skills, abilities and knowledge. I consulted some of my friends who were also going through the same process. We had discussions and shared thoughts, ideas, and templates- it was only then that I finally got comfortable with developing my CV.

That fruitful exercise lead me to developing an immensely powerful CV and getting shortlisted in all the jobs I applied for. This very CV is the one that landed me four interviews during my first year in the job market. I realised back then that there was no absolute single formula for success in this area but then again it was important that you follow a certain pattern. Moving forward, I was comfortable with developing CV's and I have done so for many people and Almost all of them landed interviews in their endeavours (jobs, educational institutions, etc.). It was this success that sparked a different thought within me: that perhaps many more people could benefit from this information. Not everyone will have an opportunity to learn how to develop a CV from friends like I had, and not everyone will have time to teach themselves. It is for these reasons and more that I have developed this guide to assist you.

As I grew in my career I saw many variations of CV's. Some were good, some were horrible and yet others still had potential. I quickly realised that a CV can be a stumbling block in your career development. It may be the very reason why you either don't get invited to an interview, don't access opportunities in the right places, or even why you are stuck in a job that you don't like. Your CV is like your lawyer; you may be innocent but if your lawyer does not represent you well- you may end up in jail. If your CV does not represent you well- you may end up unemployed or even stuck in a job you hate, no matter how educated and skilled you may be.

Your CV is a mirror image of you and the clearest reflection of who you are in the eyes of an employer. Had it not been for that consultation with my friends, I don't know what would have become of me. Seeing just how crucial a CV can be in one's career compelled me to share this information.

This book will serve as a guide to lead you into developing a winning CV that won't be easily tossed aside by potential employers. It is aimed at kick-starting your career if you are new in the job market. It also aspires to improve your chances of either getting promoted or making a vertical movement in another organisation. I believe that this book will help you unlock many doors to opportunities and place you at an advantage of being shortlisted.

# CHAPTER 1

## WHY CV?

Commonly abbreviated as 'CV', Curriculum Vitae is a Latin expression denoting the course of one's life. Simply put, it is a brief document that tells the story of who you are, where you have been and what you have done. Your life experiences model you to change and become the person that you are; it is your experiences that determine your abilities and capabilities.

During job applications, you are not there to represent yourself, it is your CV that does that on your behalf. My biggest questions are: Does your CV represent you effectively? Do you see yourself when you go through your CV? If you don't see yourself then perhaps it is time to upgrade your CV to the one that effectively represents you. Your CV should reflect you; people should have a feel of what kind of a person you are just by going through your CV.

No employer is interested in knowing every single detail of a person's life so, a CV will depict only the necessary aspects of one's life. It is important that this document only contains relevant information and most importantly, information that shows how you could benefit a potential employer. The Oxford Dictionary defines a CV as, "A brief account of a person's education, qualifications and previous occupations typically sent with a job application." It reflects where you are in life in terms of what you have learned and achieved so far. In summary, a CV is a document that details your education, experience, knowledge, skills and personal information. It is a document that you use to apply for work. It is the story of your life – it is your personal brand and it is who you are.

*Your CV tells your story, it is who you are. It's your personal brand!*

## SOME KEY TERMS RELATING TO YOUR LIFE

**BIOGRAPHY**
» The story of your life

**RESUME**
» The sum up of your career.

**CURRICULUM VITAE**
» The course of your life

## RESUME

A resume only gives information about your career life, detailing in short your work experience and your education. Most professional positions requires you to submit one in application for a Job. There is a very close similarity between a resumé and a CV. A resume focuses more on your professional life while a CV is much more detailed.

## BIOGRAPHY

While a resume only depicts information about your career life, a biography details information about your whole life and it is inspired by the events of your life- From when and where you were born to where you are today, it is the history of your life. An interesting fact is that a biography can be written by yourself (Autobiography) or by someone else. For example, someone may decide to write a biography of your academic life or any single aspect of your life that has inspired them to write about it.

## CURRICULUM VITAE

A CV is generally used to apply for employment. However, this document can be used whenever you need someone to have an idea of who you are, where you have been, what experience you have and most importantly, what your capabilities are. For instance, it can be used when you want to further your studies. It is a summary of your personal information as well as your career history. It is your representative when applying for a Job and very often determines whether you land that interview or not. Since it is our subject topic, we are going to deep dive into all aspects of a CV through out this book.

## YOUR CAREER ASPIRATIONS

Everyone has their own career aspirations. One may be look-ing to get into employment now and navigate into business later, while another just wants to have an income and live a standard life. Meanwhile, others cannot settle for being aver-age, they want to achieve more, be more and have a greater impact. Whatever your aspirations may be, it is important to have clear career goals.

**The following questions may help you make your career goals clearer:**

- Are you happy with your current career?
- How long do you want to be in that job/company?
- Are you seeking possible promotion opportunities?
- What qualifications are needed at the level you are aiming for?
- Do you have the necessary qualifications?

A lot of people will simply get into employment without being clear or even being sure of what they want next. They often end up surprised when they become stuck in a job they don't like. When I started working, my career goals were simple and clear. I wanted to experience working in both the public and the private sectors, I later wanted to experience working in a pharmaceutical manufacturing environment. As much as I had clear goals, I didn't consider the skills and education that I needed in order to achieve them. Subsequently I didn't take the necessary steps to get to where I wanted to be. Needless to say that I never got there. As much as it is important to have career goals, it is just as important to take proper actions to realise your goals.

Here are some things to consider when setting your career goals:

- Be clear about where you want to be;
- Get the right skills, education and experience and
- Take direct and appropriate action.

These three things will move you forward and assist you in meeting your career aspirations. Having a vision helps you to know where exactly you want to be, what skills, education and experience are needed, as well as the action steps that will lead you there. These are discussed in a little more detail in the next section.

## THREE KEY ASPECTS IN YOUR CAREER DEVELOPMENT

 VISION

 ASSETS

 ACTION

In order to achieve success in your career, it is important to have a vision. If you don't know where you are going, you are unlikely to get there. Your vision is the one that will give you direction and you therefore need to be clear about your final goal. Secondly, you need to go all out to equip yourself with assets (education, knowledge, experience and skills) that are necessary to get you there. It simply doesn't end at accumulating assets. The final step requires taking the necessary action that will lead to the manifesting or actualising of your goal. This may mean doing applications and enquiries about what you need to do to get there, remembering that it is the small steps that will eventually get you to your goal.

*The only way to get anywhere is to*
*know where you want to be!*

## PURPOSE OF YOUR CV

From the definition of a CV, you can already see that this document serves many purposes. The most common purpose being in job application. This document must convince your employer of your employability. Your CV is meant to communicate on your behalf; it should market you to such an extent that you cannot be rejected. It needs to express to the recruiters why you are a perfect candidate for the position at hand and why you would be an asset to the company. The main purpose of your CV in job application is to **land you an interview!** Employers use your CV in a different manner as compared to yourself. Here is what they are looking for in your CV:

## A CV helps the employer to:

- Have an overview of what kind of a person you are by providing a snapshot of your career: where you have been and what skills you have gained that they can use;
- Filter unsuitable candidates;
- Find people that can improve the performance of the company and
- Identify opportunities that they can explore.

## Your CV should help you to:

- Introduce yourself;
- Tell your story: who you are, what you have done in terms of your experience and achievements;
- Market yourself: Your CV is your number one selling tool, it is your sales pitch;
- Represent you in your absence and
- Facilitate self-discovery: helps you to think about the impact you have made.

## Your CV should answer the following questions:

- Who are you?
- What education do you have?
- Where have you been in your career life?
- What have you achieved?
- What skills have you learned?
- Why are you applying for this job?

*Of all things, employers use CVs to*
*filter unsuitable candidates.*

If your CV answers all these questions and impresses the recruiters, you will most definitely receive that long-awaited call for the interview. Every business has two main goals: To solve problems and to make money. The question you should ask yourself and the question every employer want you to answer is this: How are you going to help them achieve these two goals? Your CV should tell it all and set you apart from the crowd.

*Your CV is your number one selling tool; it is your sales pitch!*

## Places where you can use your CV:

- Volunteering;
- Scholarships;
- Educational institutions;
- Research;
- Employment and
- Pursuing personal mastery.

*Your CV must set you apart from the crowd.*

Notes

# CHAPTER 2

## CAREER PATHS

There are many different types of career opportunities out there. With employment just being one of them, it is unfortunate that many people merely default to just being an employee and do not explore other opportunities. Graduates in particular default to drafting a CV and pursuing job opportunities. It doesn't have to be that way. If all of us seek employment, then who will end up being the employer?

Not everyone will find a job in a particular organisation. There are people that need to create employment opportunities for themselves as well as others in the society. Which one are you? You may be the latter, do not limit yourself. If you have been seeking employment opportunities for quite some time without any success, then perhaps it is time to explore other opportunities.

*THINK OUTSIDE THE BOX*

Below are types of employment opportunities that may be available to you (obviously also depending on the type of qualifications you have). Take time to go through them, this will help you to make a sound decision about the kind of employment you require.

## FULLTIME EMPLOYMENT

This is the type of employment where you are required to work regular hours, usually an average of 40 hours per week depending on the contract agreed upon between you and your employer. The advantage of this kind of employment is that you get a regular income on a monthly or weekly basis as per your agreement. You may also get employee benefits such as medical aid, overtime allowance, paid leave, sick leave, bereavement, compassionate leave, parental leave and public holiday pay while still receiving your regular income. The disadvantage is that you don't have much free time to do other things. If you are an ambitious person and love exploring other opportunities outside of fulltime employment, this type of employment may leave you time-deprived. This is the type of employment that the majority of employees belong to.

## PART TIME EMPLOYMENT

This is the type of employment where you work less hours per week on a regular basis. You will usually receive the same wages and benefits as a full-time employee, though on a pro rata or proportionate basis according to the number of hours that you work. With part-time employment you get to have more time on your hands that you can use for other things. The wages are proportional to the amount of time you invest in the company but then again, it leaves you with more time to explore other opportunities that can bring you more income or more freedom.

> *Part time employment may not make you financially rich, but you will have more time to explore other opportunities.*

## CASUAL EMPLOYMENT

Casual employees are engaged on an irregular basis according to the business demands that the employer has. There is no expectation of on-going work by either the employer or employee. You as an employee have no obligation to accept offers of work. No sick or annual paid leave and no obligation to provide notice of ending your employment, subject to the type of contract you have signed. Working engagements are not guaranteed and you may find yourself with no income on certain months. I have participated in this kind of employment before and I found that, when juxtaposed alongside my full-time job, it was lucrative because I got paid for each hour that I worked. This type of employment is full of uncertainties and it is better to pursue when you have another regular income.

> Casual employment is full of uncertainties; it is better to pursue along with a full-time job or a business that brings in regular income.

## FIXED TERM CONTRACT

This is employment on a fixed term basis, and it means that you are employed for a specific period of time, to perform a specific task or a particular project or even to substitute an employee on leave. As an employee on a fixed term contract, you work full-time or part time depending on your contract. You are entitled to some of the benefits that permanent employees enjoy but only for the period of your contract. For example, you may be entitled to paid leave and sick leave proportionally to the period of your contract.

*You are not guaranteed employment at the end of your contract term when you are a contract worker*

## APPRENTICESHIP AND TRAINEESHIP

This is for students who are working towards a nationally recognised qualification. You must be formally registered as such and there must be a contract between a registered training provider, the employer and yourself the employee. Your employer pays you a trainee wage according to their rate.

## COMMISSION AND PIECE RATE EMPLOYEES

In this type of employment, you are paid a piece rate or commission after you have achieved the goal that has been agreed upon. This means that you get paid for the results you have produced as opposed to a monthly, weekly or hourly rate. In essence, no results means NO pay. Some companies do however offer a basic wage plus commission, meaning that you will receive a basic wage topped up with commission depending on your performance for the period. This can be very lucrative if you are a high performer. This type of employment is more commonly found in sales. If you find yourself in this type of employment, you need to keep some savings to help you on rainy days.

> *You will not get paid if you do not achieve the target/goal while you are a commission worker.*

## SELF-EMPLOYMENT

You get to choose when you want to work, where you want to work from, how long you want to work and how much money you want to earn. Working for yourself comes with freedom to do whatever you want to do, on your own terms and in your own time. You solve problems and get paid for it. Most people that are self-employed own businesses that are only big enough for themselves and they don't need to employ staff. The problem with self-employment is that you are the sole service provider and services cannot be provided when you are unable to do so, for example, you might not have an income when you are sick because you won't be able to provide services.

## ENTREPRENEURSHIP

*Entrepreneurs are the solution to unemployment.*

These are the people that bring solutions to societal problems; they add value to people's lives and create employment. As an entrepreneur you are an innovator and you bring new ideas, goods and services to the market with the aim of making life better. You bear the risks associated with the business, but you also get to enjoy the rewards which could be fame, growth opportunities and making lots of money. Being an entrepreneur comes with high risk, but it can also be rewarding to you, to other people and to the economy. The more entrepreneurs we have, the more jobs can be created. The future of each country depends on entrepreneurs to better the lives of its people through better services and in creating employment. These people are the solution to the unemployment problems that countries are facing.

*Entrepreneurs provide solutions to societal problems, bringing value and employment to the lives of the people.*

## Advantages and disadvantages of employment types

| Employment type | Advantages | Disadvantages |
| --- | --- | --- |
| Full time employment | Regular wages. Employment benefits. | Time poverty. |
| Part time employment | Employment benefits. More time to explore other opportunities. | Partial income. |
| Casual employment | You can make more money if you have another regular income or a business on the side. | No work, no income. No guaranteed work engagements. Proportional income. |
| Fixed term contract | You can explore other opportunities at the end of the contract term. You don't have to be there for a long time. | When the contract expires, you might become unemployed again. The company decides if they need to hire you again after the contract or not. |
| Apprenticeships and traineeship | Working a few hours a week according to the company's demands or a negotiated contract. You will gain great work experience. | You may be paid a little or no salary as per your agreement with the company. You will have to learn many tasks, complete assignments and work hard. |

| | | |
|---|---|---|
| Commission work | You can make big money if you sell well. Commission work can also be part-time work, giving you time to work on other opportunities. | Earning commission means you can make little or no money if you don't sell well. |
| Self-employment | Freedom of time and choice. You don't have staff; you don't have to pay wages. | There is no guaranteed income from self-employment. No income when you are not available to provide the services because no one else will. |
| Entrepreneurship | Living your purpose and pursuing your dreams. You can make large amount of money and earn great recognition. | Business typically takes time to build-up momentum. Many risks associated with starting a business. |

Table 1: summary of employment types

*There are many types of employment opportunities out there. Your job is to explore all and choose the one that is best for you...*

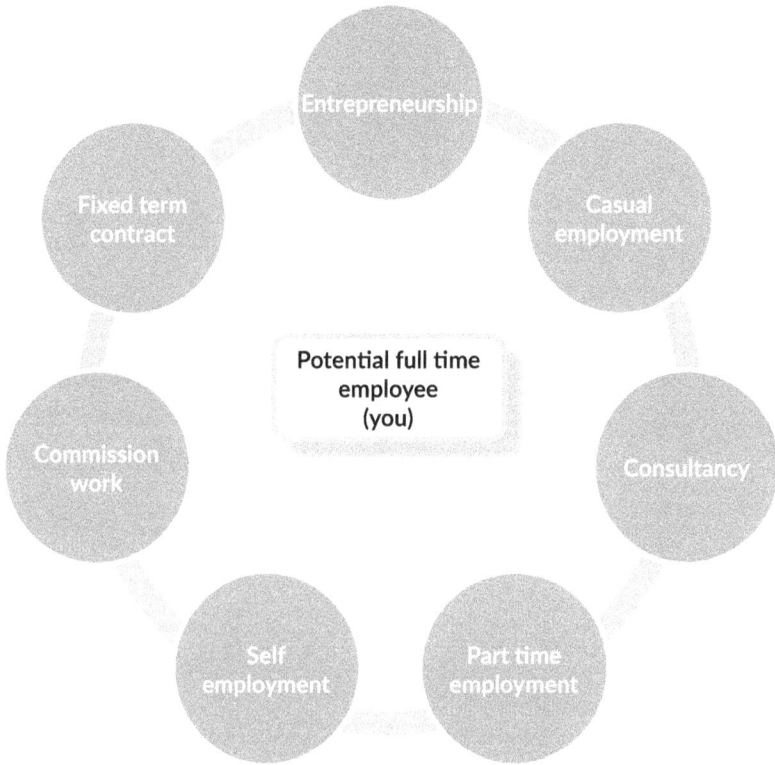

Entrepreneurship

Casual employment

Fixed term contract

Potential full time employee (you)

Consultancy

Commission work

Self employment

Part time employment

**THINK OUTSIDE OF THE BOX**

I want to challenge you to think outside of the box before you even begin with job applications. It is important to know and understand the kind of employment you are looking for, whether it will be suitable for the kind of lifestyle you want to live and if it meets your needs and requirements. **Think outside of the box!**

Notes

# CHAPTER 3

# THE RECRUITEMENT AND SELECTION PROCESS

Before a company can decide to employ someone, they first identify a gap in their services, whether it is to improve their service or to introduce a new service. All companies have a simple goal in their business, to provide value to their customers and they are seeking to deliver this value through you. As a result, there is a process that they follow in order to make sure that they recruit only the people that they believe will bring value and optimal deliverance to their customers.

*Every business exists for two reasons:*
*to solve problems and to make money.*
*Your CV must demonstrate how you*
*will help them achieve the two.*

Typically, a recruitment and selection process follows six steps. It is important that you understand the steps in the recruitment and selection process before you can start developing and sending through your CV to different employers. I am going to take you through each step of the recruitment and selection process.

# STEP 1

## The vacant job's requirements are specified

The company identifies a vacancy within their department and the manager then outlines what the job requirements will be, according to the gap that they have identified. The manager will then set out the job specification, job description, outcomes and outputs that they are looking to achieve. This step is of utmost importance as it provides direction to the type of individual who is being sought after.

Here the team also decides what sort of person they need in terms of qualifications, knowledge, skills, abilities and values that can help them deliver. The job requirements are then put into an advertisement or document that states the requirements and specifications for job applicants.

Technically, this is where the position is filled. This part is the one that tells it all. What needs to be achieved and what set of skills are required in order to deliver the output required. During this stage, the company seeks to complete the puzzle (job) and set out to find their perfect missing piece (the person) to successfully complete the puzzle. By the time they look at your CV, they'll already know if you are the missing piece they are looking for or not.

*Companies want to recruit someone that will bring value to their customers.*

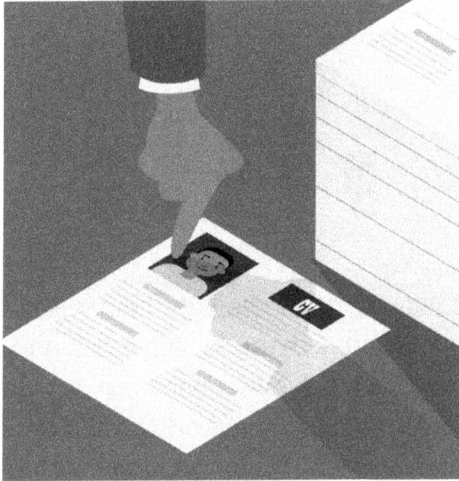

## STEP 2

### The job vacancy is communicated/advertised

The job vacancy is advertised or communicated through various communication channels. Advertising can take place through printed media (newspapers), online, notice boards, through word of mouth or even on social media. Depending on the company's needs, they may choose to advertise only internally, externally or both. After the vacancy is advertised, people will start sending their CV's and applications for the position. A closing date and application procedures are also given in the advert. Though assumed to be obvious, many companies will indicate that no late applications will be accepted. All applications received will be placed somewhere safe while waiting for the selection process to take place.

# STEP 3

## Applicants are shortlisted

After the closing date, the hiring team looks at all the applications that have been received for consideration. Depending on the number of applications received by the company, the hiring team will use different selection criteria to search for the best suitable candidates they can shortlist.

The applications that best meet the job requirements are selected, shortlisted and the applicants are then invited for an interview. Depending on the company's criteria regarding the pool of candidates they need in order to deem their selection process successful, they will screen all applications (while removing the least qualifying applicants) until they have the desired number of candidates that they are looking for. The company may also conduct a selection test if they have a high number of selected candidates in order to reduce the number and select the best candidates. The top candidates are then short-listed and invited for an interview.

### FACT

Only 3% of CV's make it through the first round of the selection process

# STEP 4

## Top applicants are interviewed

The short-listed candidates are interviewed. The interview will typically be conducted by either one interviewer or a panel of interviewers over one or more interviews. The company's interviewers will compare their interview scores or feelings about the applicant's suitability. The overall top candidate is identified (it could be one or more) depending on the needs and requirements of the organisation. Some companies use various methods of selecting candidates in addition to the interview process. You may also have to go through a competency assessment test, suitability assessment, medical fitness tests and other tests if the company decides it is necessary.

# STEP 5

## Checks are done and references are called

A company may decide whether to appoint a certain candidate or not, based on a reference check result. Every company has a set rule about which references or checks they conduct, these may include:

- Your criminal record;
- Your credit history;
- Your educational qualifications;
- Your last working or educational reference and
- At least one or more working or character references.

## STEP 6

**An offer is made**

Once a decision to appoint an applicant is made, the lucky winner of their 'dream-job' will get a call and a job offer, followed by an offer letter and further discussions. Companies may choose to let the other applicants know that they were unsuccessful, though most companies do not do this. The company and applicant agree on a salary, benefits and a starting date.

There are many factors to be considered by companies before they can appoint you. Things such as your cost towards the company. I have been to interviews where I performed so well, but later received letters stating that I was unsuccessful and didn't get the job. When I made further enquiries , I found that it had not been related to my interview but rather due to the fact that the company couldn't afford my services; firstly because of my work experience and secondly because of the amount I was already earning. Unfortunately, if you are already earning above their budget, the company won't even bother making you an offer. If you possess a sought after skill, the company will off course go out of their way to have you in their team- while also considering the losses they may encounter by letting you slip through their fingers.

Notes

# CHAPTER 4

## STEP BY STEP GUIDE TO DEVELOPING A PROFESSIONAL CV

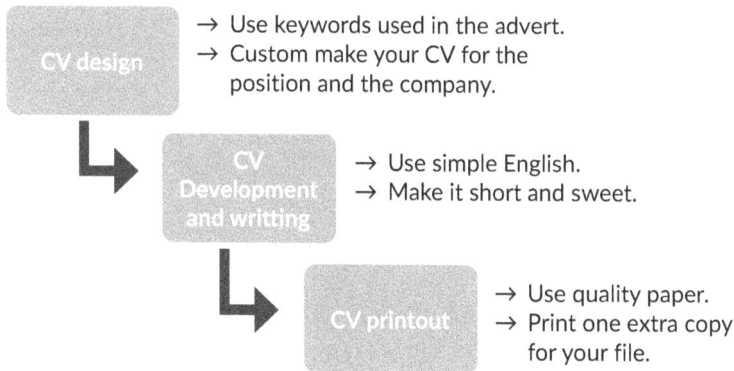

**CV design**
→ Use keywords used in the advert.
→ Custom make your CV for the position and the company.

**CV Development and writting**
→ Use simple English.
→ Make it short and sweet.

**CV printout**
→ Use quality paper.
→ Print one extra copy for your file.

We have already spoken about the fact that a CV is a personal document; it is about you - who you are as a person, what you have accomplished and overcome personally in your career and what life experiences have shaped you. Your CV is who you are, it is your own personal brand!

Your CV should be custom made for each specific job in a specific organisation. It should be in line with the job specification and description on the advertisement. It should highlight (without being dishonest) your skills and abilities that align

with what is listed in the job advertisement. It should reso-
nate with the company values, for example, if problem solving
skills are part of the job description then you should consider
having that in your CV, without giving false information.

You must consider using keywords that are featured in the
original job advertisement as it makes your CV relevant to
the company and makes life easier for the hiring team. Minor
mistakes in your CV can get you rejected particularly if the
position requires attention to detail as a skill. There should be
a balance between professionalism and personality. It helps to
include a personal summary in your CV as not only does it give
a personal touch, but it may also give a glimpse of important
information about your life that you cannot include in your CV.

*FACT*

A recent study found that a recruiter
spends a minimum of approximately
7seconds when browsing through a CV.

Now that you know what a Curriculum Vitae is, hopefully you
can better understand the different types of employment
opportunities available to you as well as the steps in the
recruitment and selection process. You should also by now
know what type of employment will best suit your lifestyle or
at least have an idea. I am now going to take you through the
process of developing a TOP NOTCH CV, the one that won't
be put aside by recruiters, A CV that will lead you straight to
your dream job.

As mentioned in the introduction, this book will serve as an
essential guide to help you develop a Curriculum Vitae of an
extremely high standard so that you have the best chance of
securing employment. Alas...**let's get into it!**

## STEP 1

**Tailor make your CV for the position and the organisation**

Your CV should always be custom made; this means that your CV needs to be revised every time you apply for a new position. Take your time in ensuring that it is relevant for the specific position in that specific company. It needs to highlight the education, experience and skills related to the position. It should show the specific values and attributes that are in line with the company you are looking to join. Also remember that your CV represents you, you are your CV so this document must represent you effectively.

## STEP 2

**Language and presentation**

Most people do not spend as much time and effort as they should on creating their CV'S, not realising that only a professional, high quality and well-presented CV will stand out from the rest. Employers receive a plethora of CV's for an advertised job, so it is especially important to create a good impression to capture their attention. Your CV is the first chance you get to make a lasting first impression on a potential employer. A top-quality CV will considerably boost your chances of getting a call to an interview, so it is worth spending the time and effort on the content and presentation. It may sound silly to say this, but it is important that your CV is written in clear English.

## STEP 3

## CV Design

Decide what you want your CV to look like, work on the graphics and type it professionally. Save the dramatic opening pages and long stories for your journal. If you can't type or aren't confident in your ability to produce a quality product, ask for help from professional CV writers. You can also purchase a CV design from the internet and choose which design best suit your needs. Having a poorly designed CV may cost you your dream job and deprive you of the life you so badly desire. There are professional CV specialists dedicated to helping people develop professional CVs, you may opt to use their services if you are not comfortable in your ability.

## STEP 4

## CV Development and writing

Now that you know what you would like your CV to look like, you can start developing your top-notch CV that will **not** be tossed aside easily by potential employers. Make it short and sweet, a maximum of three pages if possible. Ask someone to proof-read it for you and correct spelling mistakes. Again, if you are not comfortable developing your own CV, ask professional CV developers for help, especially if you are not sure about the content and the flow. You want a CV that will stand out and won't be tossed aside.

## STEP 5

## CV Printout

Have your CV printed on good quality paper. You should have a printed and an electronic version as the latter allows for easy revision when applying for new positions. Many job applications are now done online, and some companies only accept electronic CV's. Make sure you have copies of your qualifications ready so that you can submit them when you need to do so. Most people have a CV printed out that they submit every time they apply for a position. This idea can work if you are new in the job market but if you are looking for a promotion or a career change then it could be ineffective. Your CV should change as much as you do; it reflects who you are, where you have been and where you are now.

## WHAT TO WRITE ON YOUR CV

### 1. PERSONAL DETAILS

This should include your names, address, contact details (phone number and email address), date of birth and your gender. You may add your nationality if you wish but it is not an obligation. You may consider adding a headshot (photograph) if you wish to but it is also not necessary.

There is no need to include your height, weight, or eye colour unless that specific job requests that information.

## 2. PERSONAL STATEMENT/ SUMMARY (A SHORT PARAGRAPH ABOUT YOURSELF)

This is optional but it can be highly effective in summarising your areas of expertise and strengths. It is good to include your enthusiasm about your line of work as well as your motivation towards the industry. You may also include what you are seeking to achieve as well as your inspirations .Remember to use keywords - keep it brief and concise.

### PERSONAL SUMMARY EXAMPLE

*"I am a pharmacist with experience in the hospital, retail, manufacturing and distribution sectors. I am goal orientated and hardworking. I get inspired and motivated by success hence I strive to achieve success in everything I do. I believe in education, not just formal education but also in the transfer of skills between individuals. My motto is* **'Do it right or not at all'.** *I give my best in everything I do. Excellence is the bare minimum for me".*

## 3. EDUCATION AND QUALIFICATIONS

Write these in chronological order, starting from the most recent qualification to the oldest, a brief list of schooling, college and university qualifications as well as any other qualifications. If you are currently studying for a qualification, mention it together with the results achieved so far.

E.g. 2009: B. com accounting degree (cum-laude)
University of the north

## 4. WORK EXPERIENCE/ EMPLOYMENT HISTORY

State any previous working experience that you have had that is relevant to the job you are applying for. Mention part-time jobs you did in order to gain experience. Start with your current or last employer and move backwards. You should include the dates of employment, name of employer, job title with that employer, nature of the business, duties and responsibilities as well as achievements. Try not to leave gaps in your employment history because those gaps will need to be accounted for. For example, if you stopped working in order to focus on your studies, you need to indicate that.

**When detailing your work experience, it is expected that you include the following:**

- Date that you started at your previous job(s);
- Amount of time that you spent at that job;
- Your Job tittle in that organisation;
- Date of employment termination;
- Reason for termination;
- Street address of the organisation and
- Contact details of the employer for reference checks.

E.g.
January 2010 to December 2010 (One year)
XYZ South Africa (Soweto Branch)
ICT Manager
Reason for leaving: Career enhancement

## 5.  INTERESTS AND OTHER ACTIVITIES

This is optional but it gives you a chance to portray something about your personality.

Keep it simple, mention what you do in your free time and note any achievements.

E.g.
Attending personal development seminars
Jogging
Construction of puzzles
Reading motivational books

## 6.  KEY SKILLS

Include any skills that you have obtained such as administration skills, technical skills, computer skills, Leadership skills, time management, communication skills. This is often the most neglected part of the CV, yet it is the most important one. This is in short, what recruiters are searching for in a candidate. Mention skills that are relevant to the job and most importantly, skills that you will be able to demonstrate.

## 7.  KNOWLEDGE OF LANGUAGES

List all the languages you are familiar with as well as your level of proficiency in the language. This will place you at an advantage if you are applying for a position in places where there is a language more common than English.

## 8. REFERENCES

You need to write the details of your references on your CV. Their names, contact details, their organisation as well as their position. Make sure you know your references and that they know you very well. Always ask your references for permission to use them as a reference on your CV. One thing I love to do is ask someone to call my references and ask them about me. This way I get to know what they will say when they get a call from my potential employer.

Ms S. Khosa
Finance Manager
XYZ Career Solutions
0110236544

---

### Fundamentals of A CV

Personal Information
Contact Details
Personal Statement
Relevant Educational qualifications and Certifications
Relevant Work or Volunteer Experience
Professional Registrations or Licences
Relevant Skills
References

---

## DO'S AND DON'TS ON YOUR CV

### ☑ DO...

- Highlight headings so that they stand out;
- Become clear and concise;
- Use bullet points to focus on key points, rather than large blocks of text;
- Make sure it is neat and precise;
- Use a confident tone and a positive language;
- Check your spelling and grammar;
- Print your CV on a good-quality paper and
- Provide honest information.

### ☒ DON'T...

- Bury important information;
- Use poor grammar;
- Have unexplained gaps in employment;
- Include your medical history;
- Mention your criminal status;
- Have more than three pages and
- Submit your CV without having it checked by someone neutral.

## TIPS ON DEVELOPING A WINNING CV

- Keep track of the flow
- Use as few words as possible
- Be concise
- Use keywords that they used in the advert
- Proofread several times

# THE TOP-NOTCH CV

## CURRICULUM VITAE OF KHOSA SHARON

**Personal details>>**

**Surname:** Khosa
**First names:** Sharon
**S.A identity number:** xxxxxxxxxxxxxx
**Gender:** Female
**Race:** African
**Contact number:** xxxxxxxxxx
**E-mail address:** xxxxxxxxxxxxxxx
**Postal address:** xxxxxxxxxxxxxx
**Physical address:** xxxxxxxxxxxxxxx
**Home language:** Xitsonga
**Other languages:** English, Xhosa, Zulu, Setswana and Tshivenda.

**Education>>**

2018    Advanced diploma in management
        XYZ business school
2017    Certificate in Advanced project management
        ABC Training Academy
2016    B.Pharm Degree
        UMI university
2013    Grade 12 national certificate
        VDG secondary school

**Work experience>>**

2019/01-present    **TQR Medical Distributors**
                   **Position:** Pharmacist
                   **Duties and responsibilities**
                   · Picking of stock
                   · Fridge stock delivery review
                   · Reconciling Stock returned from customers
                   · Temperature monitoring

2018/10-2018/12    **Elite Pharmacy**
**Position:** Pharmacist
**Duties and responsibilities**
- Re-packaging of medicine
- Dispensing and Counselling of patients
- Manufacturing and Compounding of pharmaceutical products

2017/01- 2017/12    **Ezulwini hospital (Soweto)**
**Position**
Pharmacist intern
**Duties and responsibilities**
- Dispensing and patient counselling
- Procurement and distribution of stock
- Management of pharmaceutical stores

**Achievements>>**

2008    **TQR Medical distributors**
Employee of the year 2019

**Developed skills>>**

- Excellent communication skills
- Project management
- Leadership, team building and planning
- Conflict management and resolution
- Presentation and training skills

**References>>**

1. Mahlangu D. (Mr.)
   Managing Director
   TQR Medical Distributors
   Tell: xxxxxxxxxx
   Cell: xxxxxxxxxx

2. Zulu O.  (Ms)
   Pharmacy manager
   Elite pharmacy
   Tel: xxxxxxxxxx
   Cell: xxxxxxxxxx

3. Nkuna Q. (Mrs.)
   Responsible Pharmacist
   Ezulwini Hospital
   Tell. xxxxxxxxxx
   Cell: xxxxxxxxxx

# Curriculum Vitae of Sharon Khosa

## SHARON KHOSA
123 Moletsane street
Phone: 011 322 4242
E-mail: sharon@elitesuccess.co.za
Website:  www.elitesuccess.co.za

I am a pharmacist with experience in the hospital, retail, manufacturing and distribution sectors. I am goal orientated and hardworking. I get inspired and motivated by success hence I strive to achieve success in everything I do. I believe in education, not just formal education but also in the transfer of skills between individuals. My motto is '**Do it right or not at all**'. I give my best in everything I do. Excellence is the bare minimum for me.

### PERSONAL DETAILS

ID No: xxxxxxxx
Race: African
Gender: Female
Home language: Xitsonga

### EDUCATION

2018: Advanced diploma in management
XYZ Business School

2017: Certificate in advanced project management
ABC Training Academy

2016: Bachelor of pharmacy degree
UMI University

2014: Grade 12 National Certificate
VDG secondary school

### LANGUAGES

| Language: | Write: | Speak: |
|---|---|---|
| English | Good | Good |
| Afrikaans | Fair | Fair |
| Zulu | Good | Good |
| Sotho | Fair | Good |
| Xhosa | Fair | Good |

## WORK EXPERIENCE

2019/01-present    **TQR medical distributors**

**Position:** Pharmacist

**Duties and responsibilities:**
- Picking of stock
- Fridge stock delivery review
- Reconciling Stock returned from customers
- Temperature monitoring

2018/10-2018/12    **Elite Pharmacy**

**Position:** Pharmacist

**Duties and responsibilities:**
- Re-packaging of medicine
- Dispensing and Counselling of patients
- Manufacturing and Compounding of pharmaceutical products

2017/01- 2017/12    **Ezulwini Hospital (Soweto)**

**Position:** Pharmacist intern

**Duties and responsibilities:**
- Dispensing and patient counseling
- Procurement and distribution of stock
- Management of pharmaceutical stores

| KNOWLEDGE AND SKILLS | HOBBIES |
|---|---|
| Microsoft Office | Soccer |
| Unisolve system | Scrabble |
| Rx solution | Reading |
| Microsoft Teams | Puzzles |
| Project Management | |

## REFERENCES

1. Mahlangu D. (Mr.)
   Managing Director
   TQR Medical Distributors
   Tel: xxxxxxxxxx
   Cell: xxxxxxxxxx

2. Zulu O. (Ms)
   Pharmacy Manager
   Elite Pharmacy
   Tell: xxxxxxxxxx
   Cell: xxxxxxxxxx

3. Nkuna Q. (Ms.)
   Responsible Pharmacist
   Ezulwini Hospital
   Tell. xxxxxxxxxx
   Cell: xxxxxxxxxx

# CV PREPAREDNESS CHECKLIST

Ticking all boxes on this table means that your CV is complete, and you are ready to go ahead on hunting for your dream Job.

| | |
|---|---|
| My CV is three pages or less in length | |
| My CV is written in clear and simple English | |
| I had someone check my CV for spelling mistakes | |
| My CV has my name on the front | |
| My CV has my contact details (telephone, cell phone and email address) | |
| My CV has my personal statement that says who I am and what I want | |
| My CV showcase my education, qualifications and skills clearly | |
| My CV includes my valuable work experience | |
| My CV has details about my hobbies and interests | |
| I have had my CV typed out and printed neatly | |
| I have an electronic copy of my CV | |
| I have all my certificates and references ready for when an employer request them | |
| My CV is a true reflection of my course of life | |
| I am proud of my CV | |

Notes

# CHAPTER 5

## HOW TO EARN
## A COMPETITIVE ADVANTAGE

Recruiters receive a large number of CV's and this isn't surprising considering the rate of unemployment. So, when you hand in your CV in an application for a job, bear in mind that there are hundreds if not thousands of CV's that the recruiters need to go through in order to select a suitable candidate. You need to ensure that you earn a competitive advantage and that your CV is not overlooked and tossed aside by recruiters.

Competitive advantage is an attribute that makes you a preferred candidate. It sets you apart from the crowd and assists the recruiters to easily spot the difference between you and the others. It highlights your ability to perform better than other candidates on the job. You need to have this advantage. Ask yourself: What makes me stand out? What would compel a company to choose me and not someone else? There are many aspects that can award you this advantage. The main question you should ask yourself is: what unique attributes do I possess that the recruiters may like? Have a look at your personal qualities, your qualification(s), your education, your experience(s), your knowledge and skills as well as your capabilities.

The competitive advantage pyramid

## TYPES OF COMPETITIVE ADVANTAGE

### ACADEMIC ADVANTAGE

What education do you have that may place you at an advantage of being shortlisted? Let's say for example you are applying for an internship position. What makes you different from other candidates with the same listed qualification?

*Competitive advantage is an attribute that
makes you stand out from the crowd and become
the preferred candidate amongst others.*

Education doesn't only refer to formal education; it also refers to anything that you are exposed to in order to become a better person. Personal development activities that you take yourself through can place you at a great advantage. Not only will it enable you to present yourself well; it will also show potential employers that you are dedicated to personal and professional growth. For example, if you have been through communication and leadership trainings, you may find yourself at an advantage of getting a job compared to someone who has not.

## EXPERIENTIAL ADVANTAGE

Having experience means that the company will have to do less training and that you will be more productive within a short period of time. But then again, the more experience you have the more the company might have to pay you for your skills so this will not always place you at an advantage, it all depends on what the company's strategy is. They may either look at hiring a few highly experienced employees at a higher cost or to hire more of less-experienced employees at a lower cost. Let's say you are applying for an internship position; you will be more likely to land an interview if you have work experience as a student, whether you were mentoring other students or whether you had a part time job to help look after yourself during your student years. You have a great advantage compared to someone with only a degree or diploma.

## COST TO COMPANY

Your lack of experience may work to your advantage if the company is looking to hire someone with no experience. How relevant are your skills and who are you competing with? Can your skills be easily replaced by technology? With the Fourth Industrial Revolution underway, a lot of companies are looking to replace people with technology. The company will always consider the cost of hiring you versus hiring someone else or using technology to achieve the same objective. Less experience is associated with lower cost to the company whereas the opposite is true for highly experienced candidates.

## BENEFITS VERSUS VALUE

Any company's main concern will be to find out how you are going to help move them forward. In other words, can you deliver what they are looking for? This will depend on who the employer is and what their needs are. Every company is in business for two reasons; to solve problems and to make money. They exchange value for money. Do you have what it takes to help them achieve the two? If so then your CV should demonstrate that.

What is the company all about? What life problems are they solving? Which of your skills are they in desperate need of? How are you going to make life better both for the company and the customer? Answer these questions successfully and you will definitely get that call for an interview. The company is looking for either the benefits or the value that you are bringing with you.

# STRATEGIES OF ACHIEVING COMPETITIVE ADVANTAGE

## MOVEMENT STRATEGY

The biggest mistake that many people make is to stay in one company, in one position for a long period of time. This is the biggest dream killer for many employees. Every employee needs to have a strategy of how they are going to navigate their employment route. Staying in one company for a long time kills motivation; you end up going to work only because you have to. It's only through having a clear strategy that you'll have clear movement goals. Once you get into the position, you should already be on the lookout for other opportunities either in the company or elsewhere. It is through movement that you get to gain experience and grow professionally and this will give you a massive competitive advantage.

## UP-SKILL STRATEGY

One way in which you can prevent yourself from reaching a ceiling in your career is to never stop learning. Upgrade your current education, get a new qualification altogether, learn a new skill or continue working on your existing skills. Learning a new skill will place you at a great advantage and help you to migrate into a new career when you reach a ceiling or when you feel stuck and want to do something different.

## POSITION STRATEGY

Do not get comfortable being in the same position forever. Human beings are changing organisms, they are meant to learn and grow. When you are stuck in one place, you get contained in a circle and the reality is that you can only grow as big as the circle you are confided in. Always strive to move to a higher level. This will give you a massive competitive advantage. Always look for bigger opportunities and position yourself properly to move in an upward direction.

*CHANGE = GROWTH = PROGRESS*

## WHO IS YOUR COMPETITOR?

It is of utmost importance to always ask yourself who you are competing with. For example, when we apply for jobs, our biggest competitors are other candidates. As soon as we get into that specific employment our biggest competitor is change. Everything changes and this includes the need(s) of the people we serve. When the needs of the customers change, the needs of the employer also changes. Change will also inform what the company requires from you. Technology has brought so many changes to the way we do things, the way we interact with each other as well as what our customers need from us.

Employers are faced with the challenge of striving to be relevant in such a way that they are always assessing their needs. Through this process they also assess if they need you. If you are stuck in one place without an awareness of this, you will be thrown out of the job market. Your competitive advantage must be reflected in your CV. For the longest time, it looked like the biggest competitor for the newspaper is other newspapers. Only recently has it become clear that their biggest competitor is the internet. Don't stay comfortable where you are, be innovative and always look for ways to improve yourself. You are in competition with change.

*THE BIGGEST COMPETITOR*
*FOR YOUR JOB IS CHANGE.*

## YOUR COMPETITIVE ASSETS

Companies are not looking for an ordinary person who can deliver what everyone else can. They are looking for a rare gem, someone that will add value to their company. What unique skills do you have that makes you an asset for the company?

How valuable are the services that you are delivering, and can the company do without them? Could it be that you are NON-IMITABLE? Can someone do exactly what you do at a better cost? When I started working as a pharmacist, pharmacy was a sought-after skill. There were fewer pharmacists, meaning that there was a high demand for the skill. Because there was a high demand, a new qualification was introduced: that of pharmacist assistants and it wasn't too long until we had an oversupply of the skill. Today, as much as pharmacist assistants cannot completely do what a pharmacist does, companies opt to work with less pharmacists and more pharmacist assistants because they are affordable. Are you NON-SUBSTITUTABLE? - how difficult is it to replace you? Is your skill so rare that the company may not be able to let you go? The more valuable and rare, the greater your competitive advantage is. Also, if you are easily replaceable and substitutable, the more your competitive advantage decreases.

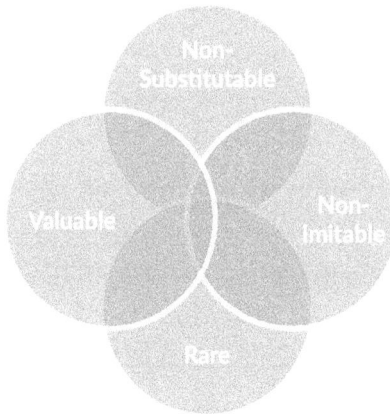

**YOUR COMPETITIVE ASSETS**

Notes

# CHAPTER 6

## GET THAT PROMOTION

It is imperative to have a goal. As soon as you get that job, you need to know for how long you intend to be in that position. What is the next vertical position and what will it take to get there? Then work your way through.

Most employers would rather promote their own employees to higher positions rather than getting someone completely new, so you always need to be ready. It is best to be ready for an opportunity which you do not end up getting than to get an opportunity that you are not ready for.

## PRODUCTIVITY

Companies are looking for output. Productivity will set you apart from other employees. Being more productive means you are increasing the speed of service. Not only will the customers be satisfied, but it will also save the company money because they will not have to pay you and other employees overtime in order to catch-up on work. A great performance is the key to a promotion. Always strive to increase your productivity. The company will make more money because the turnaround time will be less, this will allow you to serve more customers and make more money for the company.

## SIGNIFICANCE

Significance means that your presence is important in the company. Always make yourself significant in the workplace. Jump in and assist when you are done with your own duties. This will make you worthy of attention. Your presence becomes meaningful and your absence has an impact. Significance is seen in your actions. As a result of being significant, your boss becomes confident in you, believes in you and trusts you. They believe in you because they know that you can get things done. Being significant increases your value and gets people to start attaching more value to you as a person and as an employee.

When you demonstrate significance, there is no way that your managers won't notice. This is the easiest way to walk your way into your managers' heart. You become a valuable asset in your organisation. Once you crack this, you become unstoppable; the sky becomes the limit for you.

*KEYS TO BEING SIGNIFICANT*

Add value

Make a difference

Bring new ideas

## MANAGEMENT

Management doesn't only mean managing other people or being in a management position. It also means being able to manage your job and yourself. If there are any signs that you are not coping with your job, you will always be the first person to be thrown out should the company want to reduce their numbers. How do you deal with situations in the workplace, how do you respond to change, how do you deal with pressure? The following key factors will demonstrate how you manage yourself in different situations.

| Management principles that will set you apart |
| --- |
| Planning |
| Organizing |
| Directing |
| Controlling |

## COMPETENCE

This is your ability to navigate through roles successfully; it is a combination of your characteristics as well as skills that you possess. Competence demonstrates how efficient you are. Being competent is not necessarily a skill you can learn; it is rather an inherent quality that you possess as a person. But then again, competencies can be mastered through practice. Your competence level most definitely has a direct impact on your level of performance and productivity. Competence can rather be classified as a characteristic that drives one to be effective and efficient.

Competence is summoned by your knowledge, skills, behaviour and drive, causing you to act better in any specific situation.

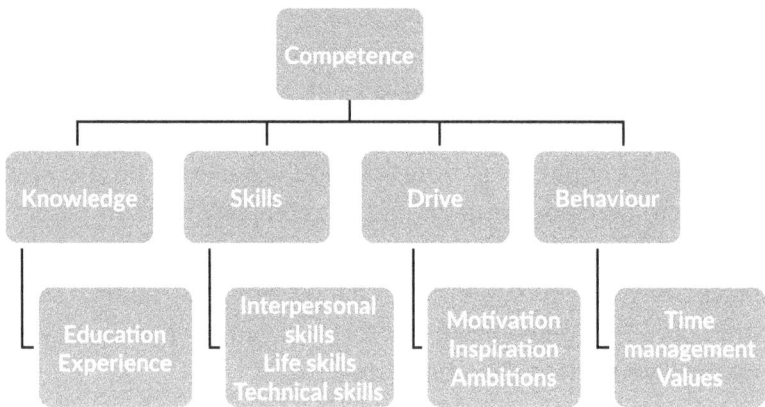

**DRIVERS FOR COMPETENCE**

## DILIGENCE

Own your work and take pride in doing good work. This tells more about your values. The saying goes that hard work pays off. If there is one thing that will take you forward, it is putting effort into everything you do as well as getting good results. Diligence will bring massive success in every project you handle; it shows that you have unquestionable work ethics and that you see any kind of work you do as being important.

## COMMITMENT

Commitment is seen in your behaviour; in the way you show up for your roles or even just showing up for work. Being committed makes work easier for other people. It is non-negotiable that when you take a job, you are making a commitment to show up and do the job. It doesn't end there; you need to commit even more to doing the job well. Commitment is a promise or agreement to be and to do.

## BE EXCEPTIONAL

This is a quality of doing, being something that is unusual or rare to see. Being exceptional is seen in your behaviour. For example, attaining an unusual skill makes you an exceptional employee. It makes you better than average. Set yourself apart from everyone else by being above average and extra ordinary. Being exceptional is as easy as doing a little extra than what is being asked or required.

## SHOW TALENT

You need to continuously demonstrate your other talents in order to be relevant. You may demonstrate other skills that you have, either natural or acquired. Become a positive presence in your workplace and get noticed. If there is another area that you are skilled in other that the one you have been employed for, you can jump in and assist if assistance is required.

## DELIVER MORE VALUE

Companies are looking for nothing other than value. If you want to climb up the corporate ladder really fast, you need to give more than what is expected. You need to deliver more than just what is in your job description. This will mean giving your maximum effort and that will differentiate you from the rest of the employees. Solve problems that others shy away from. This will really set you apart from the rest. It will obviously depend on what you classify as "adding more value."

## DEVELOP YOURSELF

The next senior position may need a different skill; you need to equip yourself to get there. Develop yourself. Learn new skills, it is through education that you can really be empowered with a new set of skills. Once you learn a new skill, it becomes difficult to stay where you are. Demonstrate your skills to prove that you are a leader. Your promotion may be lying in your ability to learn and gain a new skill. Go out there and uplift yourself.

# FIND THE PROMOTION SOMEWHERE ELSE

At times, your current organization might not be able to offer you what you are looking for. The promotion you are looking for may not be there and this becomes a sign that you need to explore opportunities elsewhere. You will need to disrupt yourself a little more by going outside of your comfort zone and explore new things elsewhere. Even better, your field may not be offering you the kind of freedom and opportunities that you need. This is another sign that you need to make your circle bigger in order to find more opportunities. Make your circle bigger, slowly but surely.

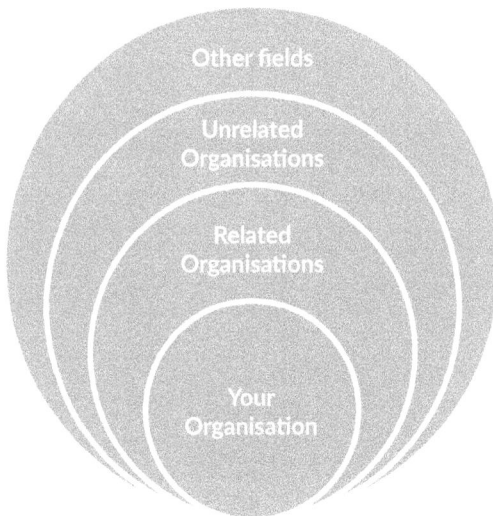

Other fields

Unrelated Organisations

Related Organisations

Your Organisation

**MAKE YOUR CIRCLE BIGGER**

## TRAITS OF PEOPLE WHO GET PROMOTED

- They have career goals
- Are team players
- Proven to be Irreplaceable
- They keep learning
- They advocate for themselves
- Show leadership potential
- They are engaged employees
- Network with the right people
- Have mentoring relationships
- Act professionally at all times
- Obtain new knowledge and skills
- Create their own opportunities

## TIPS ON GETTING A PROMOTION

- Make your boss obsolete
- Summarize work visually
- Own projects from start to finish
- Keep a positive attitude
- Show pride in your work
- Make your boss aware that you want a promotion
- Avoid office politics and gossip

## MISTAKES THAT HINDER PROMOTION

- Expecting a new title for the same job
- Continuing to do the minimum
- Not growing your skills

Notes

# CHAPTER 7

## LIVING YOUR PURPOSE

When I got into the employment world, I followed a simple routine. I would go to work, come back and prepare meals, eat and sleep. Weekends were reserved for washing and shopping in preparation for the week ahead. I went into employment with the hope of having a great life, as most of us do. But it wasn't long before it started to seem like a horribly boring life. I began asking myself if this was all there was to life? That is when I began looking for things I could do to just make my life a little more meaningful.

The search for a meaningful life lead me to selling Tupperware. I did some work on weekends to make extra money (just because I was so bored). I began visiting different places engaging in a myriad of activities which I found more fulfilling. Years later, so much has changed but I still get deeply fulfilled by interacting with people in different places.

The most pertinent question in the life of any person is, who are you? More so if you are writing your CV. This question brings clarity into one's life. When asked this question, a lot of people will usually go through their life history in chronological order, yet this question asks for more than just your life's history. This question seeks to understand your passion, your ambitions: what you like. What motivates you? What inspires you? Do you ever wake up in the middle of the night hoping that it is already the next day, because you can't wait to get going?

Most people get into a job not necessarily because they like it, but because they need the money. They grab the first opportunity that arises without even considering whether it resonates with what they are passionate about or not. There is nothing wrong with that because we all need money to make a living, but what becomes important from there is that one must have an exit strategy in place. For how long do you intend to work in that position or in that company?

Without a clear strategy it's easy to get stuck in a company that you don't value or a job you hate. Most people complain daily about how much they hate their job, yet do nothing about it. Remember it is essentially important that you are happy at work because that is where you spend most of your time. You cannot be unhappy for eight hours a day and expect to live a fulfilling life. Dissatisfaction at work tends to breed the same in personal life.

# LIVING WITH PURPOSE

Very often, we get stuck in just doing our jobs and making a living such that we forget to live a truly meaningful life. We define ourselves merely by the types of jobs that we do and totally lose out on a meaning of being our true self. There is so much to life than just making a living. There is happiness, love, peace, fulfilment and passion just to mention a few, most of which are not brought about the type of jobs that we do. This tells me that there is a gap that we need to fill, and that gap is 'purpose'. I believe that each and every one of us has a purpose in this life and that it is important for us to live our life's purpose whilst we are on this planet. You cannot do this if you do not even know what that purpose is. You need to know what you stand for and what your reason for being is, in order for you to live your purpose. In order to identify your purpose and live your passion, you need to ask yourself the following questions:

- What do I want out of life?
- What type of employment best suits my needs and requirements?
- What is my vision?
- Where am I going?
- How am I going to get there?
- What do I see myself achieving?
- What is my passion?
- What are my long and short term goals?
- What is it that makes time insignificant when I am doing it?

## WHAT DO YOU WANT?

If you are going to achieve anything in your life, it goes without saying that you need to be crystal clear about what you want. What do you want out of your job, your career, the company, out of this life? What would you consider symbolising true happiness for you? What will a deeply fulfilling life look like for you? **What do you want?**

If you're like most people, then you've been trained to adopt the mind-set below:

- Go to school
- Get a job
- Buy a house
- Get married
- Have children
- And the cycle continues with the next generation

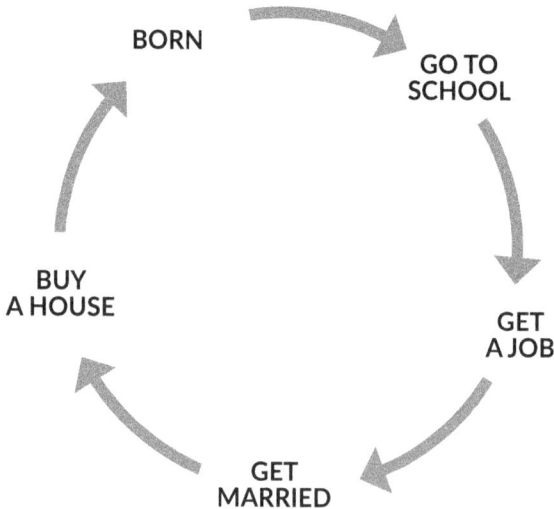

BORN

GO TO SCHOOL

GET A JOB

GET MARRIED

BUY A HOUSE

The traditional value chain system dictates that an individual should go through certain steps in their life. However, this value chain is only meant for average people and also leaves a big gap to be filled; this gap is what I call 'purpose'. Not everyone gets to uncover their purpose, it is only a few extra-ordinary people that get to uncover and live their purpose, and this is because everyone else is stuck in their comfort zone.

This system was designed for average people. Along my journey through life, I have come to realise that there are four classes of people: the below average, the average, the extra-ordinary and the ELITE. What I want to bring to your attention is that you have a choice. You can either follow this system that was designed by society and live unhappily ever after OR you can design your own. **It's up to you!**

If your value chain system does not look like this, it's not a problem; it simply means you are not playing for the average team and there is nothing wrong with being above average; there is absolutely nothing abnormal about being in the extra-ordinary or the Elite team.

There are too many gaps in this system and that is what you should use to discover yourself and how you can add to the value chain.

Human beings are individuals of change. Without change, we would be stuck in one place and we wouldn't grow, life would be a nightmare. Change yields growth and development. The same applies to employment. We constantly feel the need for change, the need to work in different spaces, serve in different ways and to just deliver a different kind of a service. What most people don't realise is that this constant need for change is a calling, a calling to live the life of your dreams, a life driven by purpose.

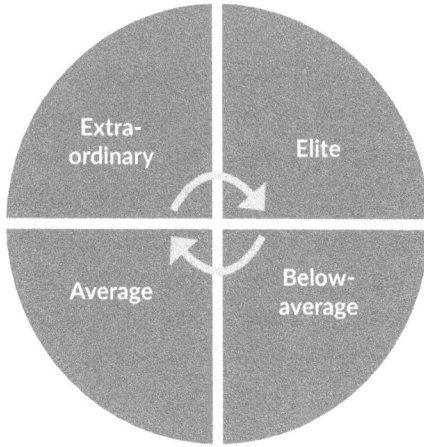

**THE DIFFERENT CLASSES OF PEOPLE**

## Below-average

These are people who are not concerned about anything in life. They do the bare minimum; they settle for anything and accept anything as it is. They never question anything; they hardly do anything to change their lives. They are poor and are comfortable with being poor.

## Average people

Average people fall into the system defined by society. They do exactly what the society defined and are comfortable being in that system. They are not so different from the below average except for their type of comfort zone. These people are the ones that will typically get a job in a company and work there for the rest of their lives or for as long as that company exist. If that company is dissolved, they will be left without a job.

## Extra-ordinary people

They put a cherry on top of what the society has served them. They modified the system to make it more comfortable for them. They will get a job, strive to move up the corporate ladder. Once they get there, they can start a small business or a ministry on the side and keep it going.

## The Elite people

These are the stars of the world. They always strive to make themselves and other people better. They never get comfortable in the game. These are the people that plant trees so that other people can enjoy the shade. They keep on changing the game, they turn the tables around. When they get to the top of their game, they start a new game. There is no such thing as a comfort zone for them.

I hope that this sheds a bright light for you to see where you are. The good thing is that you placed yourself there with an influence from the society. Just like you placed yourself there, you can remove yourself and you can place yourself in any class you desire. Life has no manual, except the one that you have designed for yourself. Since you are the author of your life manual, you can change and re-design it.

# YOUR CAREER GOALS

What are your career goals? I have mentioned before that many people go into the job without a clear plan regarding their career goals or they simply don't have goals at all. Then they wonder why they are unhappy all the time. The truth is that they get stuck, get frustrated and become unhappy because they never take the time to craft their career path and even life itself. Consider having short, medium and long term goals if you want to have a successful career and life.

Ask yourself whether your career makes you happy, does it fulfil you, does it motivate you, does it feed your spirit, do you get inspired and do you make enough money? If yes, then you should consider continuing your journey in your current career or job. If the answer is no, then you need to start searching for your purpose and making means to navigate through and live your purpose.

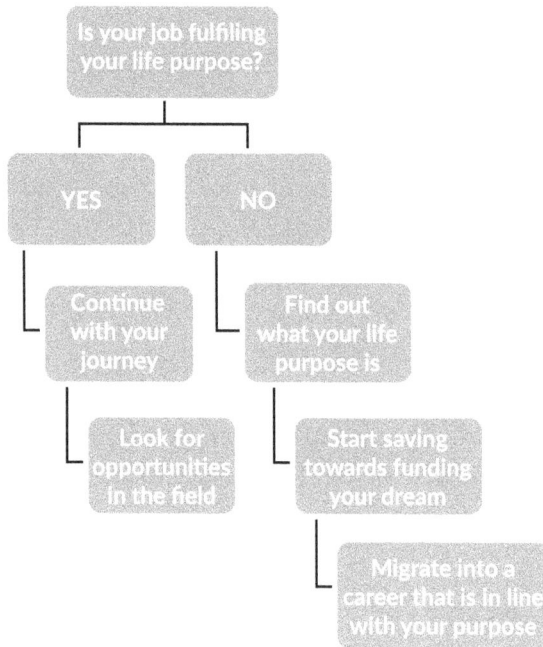

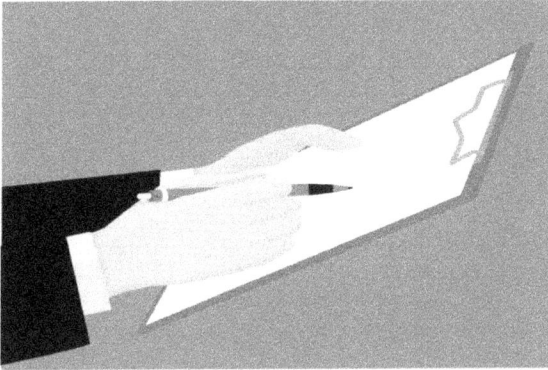

The fact that we are not going to be alive forever should serve as a wonderful motivation to live the life of our purpose. We are all aware that tomorrow is not guaranteed, but yet we live life as if life is forever. It is perhaps time to change and look at life in a different way. It is important to follow your dreams and live the life of your purpose, but it is more important that you do that now because tomorrow is not promised.

You need to discover your purpose really quickly because, if you don't do it today, it may not happen. It is urgent to live the life of your purpose. You need to be hungry to live the life of your purpose as if you are writing an urgent assignment using a borrowed pen because of the knowledge that it can be taken from you at any given time and the consequences can be tragic. Spare yourself regrets and run after your dreams.

Notes

# CHAPTER 8

## SKILLS FOR SUCCESS

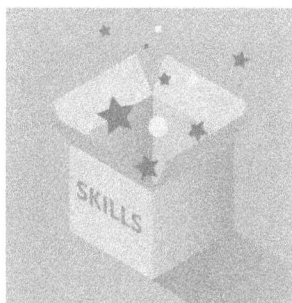

The skills section of your CV is the one that shows your employer if you have the abilities that are required in a specific role. Very often, employers pay special attention to the skills section of your CV in order to determine whether they should shortlist you or not. When I completed my degree, I didn't know what skills were needed for me to fulfil my role as a pharmacist; even worse, I didn't know what skills there were. What was more devastating is that I didn't even understand that skills were the most important component in one's career. The fact that you are reading here should already tell you that you are in a better position than I was when I completed my degree. I feel that this part is not given as much attention through our formal education and as a result, we don't know what skills we should be going for in order to make it in our career and personal lives. It is of absolute importance that you know what skills there are and then go deep within to identify what skills you possess that can help you navigate through certain tasks with ease.

Skills are obtained through education, experience, practice and even personality traits. These four things are without a doubt the most important things in life. As much as skills can be learned, there is a class of skills that comes naturally and are unique to you. These are the skills that make you who you are: they are called interpersonal skills. These are the skills that define you, how you relate to different people and how you react to different situations and circumstances. These set of skills are derived by your habits, characteristics and personal attributes. For example, having a great sense of humour, being dependable, being more adaptable. These skills are not job related, they have more to do with who you are but they make a great contribution on how you will fit like a perfect puzzle piece into the job.

Even though Personal skills are not easy to teach, one can master them if they have a strong will to become a better person. I believe that you will agree with me that everyone and especially employers needs a person or employee that is dependable and can easily adapt to different environments. Interpersonal skills are that important, they are life skills. These skills are a result of who you are, and no one can take them away from you. These are natural skills.

---

**Three most important
sections of your CV**

Education
Work experience
Skills

---

The set of skills that you possess are a result of your personal background, your education and your experiences. Skills are without a doubt, the most neglected part in most CV'S. A lot of people think it's about the list of skills but then there is more to it. Your skills define who you are in relation to the job at hand. What are the skills that you have that can enable you to deliver on that specific job.

The hiring managers will first go through your education and experience, obviously making an assessment as to what skill you may have learned. If you have the right education and experience and then they will skim through your CV to find out if you have the right set of skills. This is mainly because skills can be learned. There are hundreds of skills that are available and you may be in possession of many of them, thus it is of utmost importance to mention only the skills that are related to that specific job, focusing more on the skills that you can demonstrate. Always pick the right skills to mention, do not let your skills be a hindrance in your way of success.

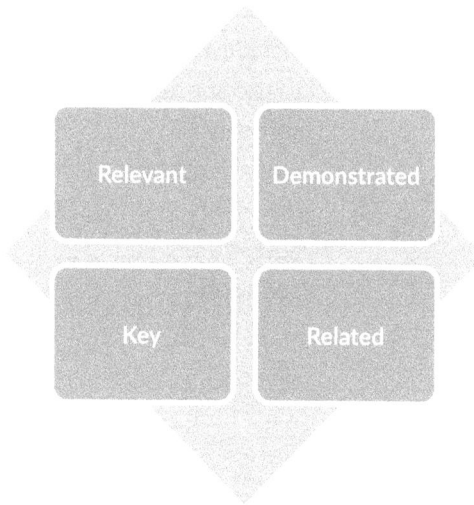

**TRAITS OF A QUALITY SKILL**

| Natural/ personal skills | Professional/ technical skills | Life skills |
|---|---|---|
| These are commonly referred to as people skills, interpersonal skills or soft skills. They are personal attributes and characteristics brought by our personal background and our life experiences. These are the skills that make you who you are. | They are specialised skills acquired through education or experience. These are the skills we need to perform on the job. These are characterised by practical abilities and specialized knowledge needed to perform tasks in a role. These include abilities to use specialised software or operate specific machinery, equipment and tools. | All other non-specialised skills fall into this category. This type Can either be learned or acquired through life experiences. They are any other skill needed that you could use together with professional skills in order to perform better in a job. |

# EXAMPLES OF IMPORTANT SKILLS

- Project management skills- Every business or company needs a project management pro. This skill ensures that things get done within time, quality and cost.
- Communication- best communicators are needed everywhere.
- Ability to work under pressure- this skill ensures continued customer satisfaction even when the workload has increased.
- Time management- the company knows they will always get value for their money.
- Conflict resolution.

# TYPES OF SKILLS THAT YOU CAN ADD TO YOUR CV- PICK ONLY WHAT IS RELEVANT TO YOU

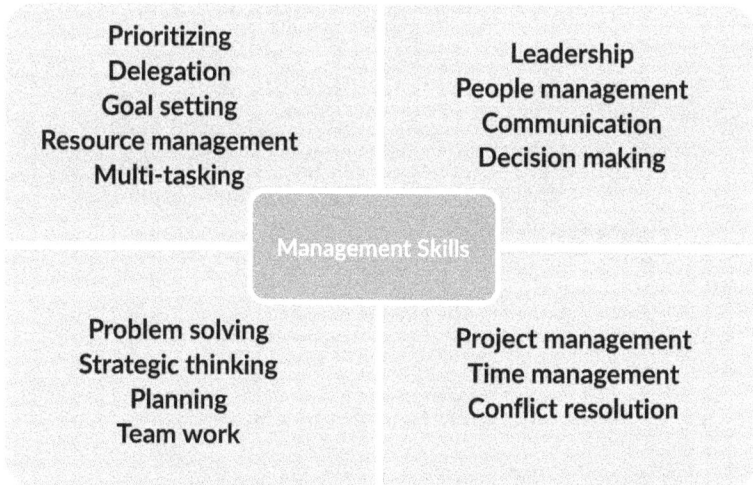

Prioritizing
Delegation
Goal setting
Resource management
Multi-tasking

Leadership
People management
Communication
Decision making

Management Skills

Problem solving
Strategic thinking
Planning
Team work

Project management
Time management
Conflict resolution

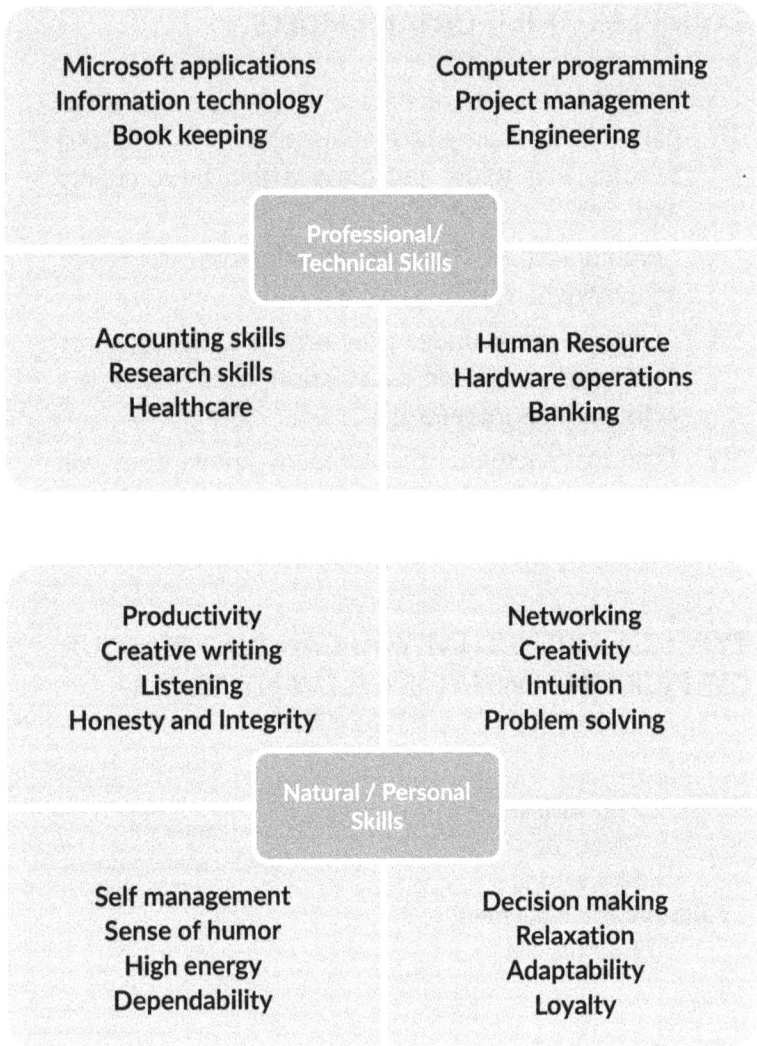

Microsoft applications
Information technology
Book keeping

Computer programming
Project management
Engineering

Professional/
Technical Skills

Accounting skills
Research skills
Healthcare

Human Resource
Hardware operations
Banking

Productivity
Creative writing
Listening
Honesty and Integrity

Networking
Creativity
Intuition
Problem solving

Natural / Personal
Skills

Self management
Sense of humor
High energy
Dependability

Decision making
Relaxation
Adaptability
Loyalty

|  |  |
|---|---|
| Risk assesment<br>Financial management<br>Leadership<br>Customer service | Decision making<br>Critical thinking<br>Planning<br>Communication |

**Business skills**

|  |  |
|---|---|
| Negotiation<br>Delegation<br>Problem solving<br>Networking | Selling and closing<br>Time management<br>Marketing<br>Project management |

**Other Skills**

| Presentation | Troubleshooting | Learning |
|---|---|---|

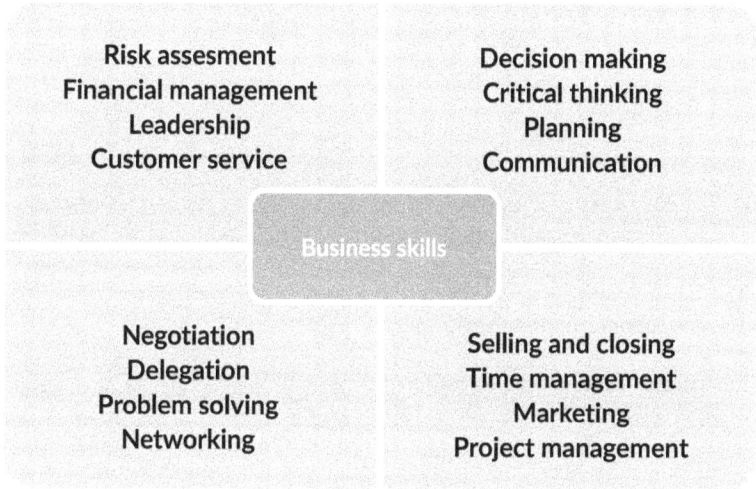

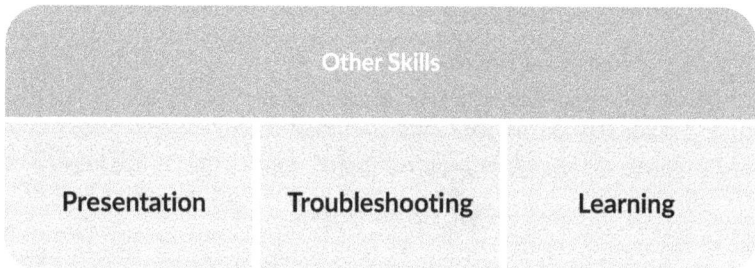

## TOP 10 SKILLS THAT RECRUITERS ARE LOOKING FOR

1. Learning
2. Innovation
3. Critical thinking
4. Problem solving
5. Communication
6. Sales and marketing
7. Creativity
8. Leadership
9. Networking
10. Emotional intelligence

## ADVERT

**Role title: Data Engineer**
**Division: Information Systems Division**

## SKILLS PROFILE

### EDUCATION

- Bachelor's Degree at the appropriate NQF level in the area of computer science, engineering, mathematics, statistics and/or a combination of these.
- Data engineering certifications such as Python, Microsoft, AWS, Hadoop, big data and cloud infrastructure.
- Project management/agile certifications such as Scrum and Prince

### WORK EXPERIENCE

- A minimum of 5 years' experience in data engineering.
- Experience with SQL and working with large scale data etc.
- Experience with distributed data processing such as Hadoop, Spark, Kafka, Hive, Nifi and Hbase is critical.
- Experience in applying machine learning techniques.
- Experience in operationalising data science solutions or similar product development experience in a high scale production environment.
- Project management or consulting experience applied in cross-functional projects.

## KNOWLEDGE

- Provide support to the ever evolving Netcare strategy of person-centred health and care. Continuously deepen the awareness of the strategy to address new challenges within the Healthcare sector, to build a competitive advantage and sustainability through the Netcare moat strategy.
- This role requires substantial expertise in a broad range of software development and programming fields, knowledge of data analysis, data-structures, algorithms and distributed computing.
- Solid understanding of physical database design principles and the system development life cycle.
- Ability to work in an agile multi-disciplined environment.
- Solution focused and strong collaborative mindset.
- Demonstrates excellent organisational skills: organised and structured.
- Outstanding problem solving and analytical skills.
- Understanding of data flows between systems, ETL and processing of structured and unstructured data within the data architecture within distributed systems (Hadoop).
- Knowledge of industry standards and organisational frameworks to produce procedures and standards.
- Knowledge of the process of scientifically and statistically evaluating data in order to determine whether it meets the quality required for projects or business processes and is of the right type and quantity to be able to actually support its intended use.
- Working knowledge and familiarity with data profiling tools.
- Knowledge of the central repository for all significant parts of data.
- Knowledge of data structuring, serialisation framework and optimisation of map reduce/spark jobs running in daily batch jobs.
- Knowledge of how to combine technical and business processes to combine data from disparate sources into meaningful and valuable information.
- The ability to plan, implement, integrate and control activities and processes to provide golden sources of contextual data.
- Knowledge of trends and developments in the health care industry.
- Knowledge of health-related policies, procedures and legislation.
- Working knowledge of multi/hybrid cloud environments and implementations.

The advert above is from a well-known private company. From the advert above, you can easily depict that all the company is looking for is your skills. They are assessing your skills based on your Education, Experience and knowledge. Life is about skills and the most important skill that one could ever have is the skill of learning more skills. Everything we do in life is about learning. It is only through learning that we can obtain a new skill.

Education brings us knowledge; our knowledge then brings us the experiences, through our life experiences which in turn teach us new skills. The skill of learning is critical.

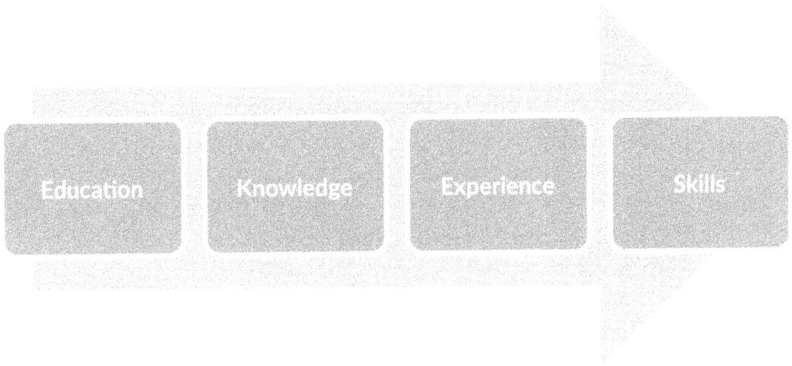

| Education | Knowledge | Experience | Skills |

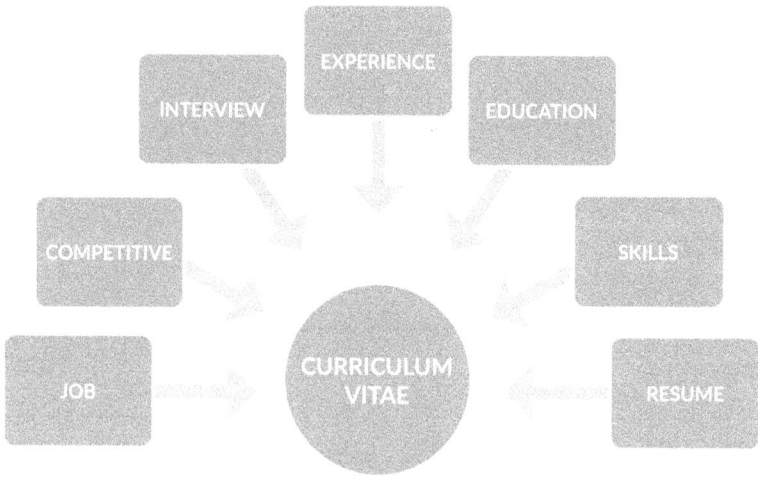

Notes

# CONCLUSION

My purpose with this book was to help you design a top-notch CV and to help you get the job of your dreams. I challenge you to reflect on a few aspects of your life such as examining what you have done and what impact you have made. If you are not happy with the findings then perhaps the time for change has come, consider what you could possibly do to change your life for the best. This is the beginning of the long-awaited journey to discovering your purpose and then living it and I am excited to be a part of your journey.

Where have you been? Where are you now? Where do you want to be? Answering these questions is the first step in living the life of your purpose. Your job may not be your life's purpose, but I believe it may be a vehicle that can get you there. Your CV is your number one selling tool, it is your sales pitch and having a winning CV will help you unlock many doors to opportunities.

Apart from designing a winning CV, there is one other thing that I need you to walk away with from this book- it is the idea of earning competitive advantage. In whatever you do, always equip yourself with assets that will give you a competitive advantage. Keep in mind that your biggest competitor is change as evidenced by the surge of the Fourth Industrial Revolution. Technology is taking over most aspects of our lives. My mission would have been accomplished if you get your dream Job and live a life driven by purpose, which I believe you will. YOUR DREAM LIFE IS CALLING YOU.

## Was this book helpful?

Leave feedback at:
sharon@elitesuccess.co.za

---

## Follow Elite Success

www.elitesuccess.co.za
@elitesuccessnow on:
facebook,instagram and twitter

---

## Follow Sharon Khosa

@sharon_khosa on instagram and twitter
@sharonthesuccesscoach on facebook